WHISPERS
IN TIME

ALSO BY KYLE NIELSON

Sharing Treasure

WHISPERS IN TIME

A poetic anthology

Kyle Nielson

40/50

FIRST EDITION

Published by UpRorr Media
Arlington, VA 22209
www.uprorr.com

Author: Kyle Nielson
Introduction: Douglas S. Carraballo
Cover Design: Kyle Nielson
Illustrations: Kyle Nielson

Library of Congress: 2023922640
ISBN-13: 979-8-9895722-0-5 (paperback)
ISBN-13: 979-8-9895722-1-2 (ebook)

Printed in the United States of America

For Lia, I didn't know my life was a blank coloring book until you started to paint it vibrantly.

For you, the reader, I'm honored to share whatever patch of road we travel together in this life.

CONTENTS

FOREWORD

Consideration One

I walked up the short staircase to the gymnasium stage in my finer clothes of the day. My eyes searched the floor for a painter's tape X directly before the microphone's metal stand. Gently placing my feet on either side of it, I looked up to see only black. Even with the bright spotlight, I thought I would see the audience, yet no one was visible. Not my friends, parents, or hundreds of other children and adults who littered the gym, each in attendance for this primary school poetry reading of third graders.

Terrified of judgment from no one in particular, perhaps from the darkness in general, words stumbled over each other as the looseleaf paper trembled in my hands. I recall thinking, I spent time on this poem, and now it's ruined. I then walked off the stage with my head low and cannot remember whether there was applause.

Does that matter if you don't believe your work is good?

My next memory of poetry was in high school. Friends would circle up at parties and attempt to freestyle with music. Impromptu poetry. I didn't join in as much as I wanted because I feared embarrassment. Not that anyone was judging me except myself. Listening to them and occasionally giving a reasonable attempt was still a blast. What little poetry I did write was teenage drama.

I heard about slam poetry in my early twenties and fell in love. The poetry was still about the drama of the day, I just let loose a little more. Poetry was now about emotions, about people, about situations, and about dreams. I shared more of it with friends and partners. Their feedback and encouragement kept me alive and moving.

A decade more experience writing poetry, and now, in my 30s, I feel no better at poetry than the 9-year-old who trembled on stage. The audience continues to be behind a thin veil of light; the nerves still linger, and I can hear the darkness whisper that I am judged for incompetence.

Well, darkness, your whispers are ever-present, and the poetry comes whether I like it or not, so I might as well share it.

Consideration Two

Both of my grandfathers wrote poetry.

One grandfather wrote patriotic poetry. He was an All-American man. He grew up in the 1920s, married a school teacher (my grandmother) when he returned from the military, frequently attended church, raised seven Mormon children (mostly boys), watched sports, and cared about their town.

My other grandfather was similar, yet so different. He grew up in the 1930s, served in the Korean War, married a Catholic woman (my grandmother) who converted when she met him, broke social norms like belching at the dinner table and signing about excrements, raised six Jewish children (mostly girls), watched sports, and cared about their town.

When I think about poetry, I think about rhyming. I enjoy a good rhyme. I don't have an exact reason for why. Perhaps it's because my grandfathers liked to rhyme in their poems.

Rhyming feels good. It's pleasant to my ears. I hope it will be for you, too.

Consideration Three

I have always had a fascination with Japanese culture. I grew up watching anime and loved the fantastical worlds they transported me into. My parents signed me up to take Karate as a kid. My brother and I played Nintendo. My parents would take us to eat sushi on birthdays. I watch Pokemon on Saturday mornings.

I wanted to be strong like a Samurai and invisible like a Ninja, so it's no surprise that I also enjoy the Haiku poetry form.

Common haikus have a 5-7-5 syllable structure in three lines, like so:

The rose may be red
and a violet may be blue,
should your eyes see true.

Anyone can write a haiku. They are simple. They are concise. And I may be preferential to rhyming, though the haiku doesn't have to rhyme. Haikus can also have a 3-5-3 syllable format. Poetic purists will say that a haiku needs a reference to the season or a cutting juxtaposition of images.

A haiku is an abbreviated form of a tanka, a 5-7-5-7-7 poem. When multiple haikus or tankas are strung together consecutively, the longer form poem is called a renga.

Further, while a haiku or a tanka is usually about mother nature, a senryu poem is another poem usually about human nature. Both a senryu and a haiku can be serious or humorous.

Knowing a little more about the style of the poems I read is something I've found fascinating, and so I share that knowledge with you (if you didn't already know).

You'll see haikus, senryus, tankas, and rengas in these pages. You'll find a mix of this poetry style with my own style. And, of course, many poems will have nothing to do with the Japanese-styled poetic structure at all.

Consideration Four

When I reflect on my poems, the same topics appear again and again:

❖ Enjoying life
❖ Analyzing pain
❖ Reframing losses
❖ Seeking development
❖ Distinguishing nuances
❖ Understanding emotions

Why are these the common topics? As you read through the poems within this book, you'll discover the answer for yourself, for the treasures found in life are challenging to identify, so we keep looking.

WHISPERS
IN TIME

INTRODUCTION

What is poetry?

It is a challenge to reflect on the nature of poetry for several reasons. Any definition, like all linguistic attempts to capture and define art, any definition is a teacup dipped into an ocean and shared amongst friends. The flavor is there, the essence potentially captured, yet the feeling will be vastly under-articulated.

I often consider poetry the bridge between music and prose. It is the world of shades and angelic shapes that brush at the edges of reality.

Poetry remains an enigmatic force, like something that scratches the outer and inner rim of the skull and sits atop your skeletal frame.

Poetry refuses to reconcile itself with any societal assurances of the known world. It is an inherently rebellious force because it cracks the façade of monotony and triviality that so characterizes our daily lives.

Poetry is an attempt to see reality for what it is and re-elevate existence to its proper, mysterious throne. It is both a fist and a satin glove caressing your face.

Those who practice poetry commune with something that the tongue falters to lick thoroughly, like the taste of sea brine and oysters, dead against the windbroken Atlantic coast that sits on the edge of your mouth... or something along those lines.

What follows is a collection of poems written by a dear friend. He is someone whom I consider a fellow madman, a companion who continuously amuses and amazes me with his resilience, persistence, and intellect.

The pen has been set to paper. The printers are running. I hope you enjoy this anthology as much as I did.

-Douglas S. Carraballo, 2023
IG: @poemsbydouglas
X: @poetbwa

SECTION 1:
PLAY AND ART

As the saying goes, *it goes without saying*, and yet here I am saying it anyway: **If you're not having fun with life, you're not living right.**

Years ago, I was walking through a museum with a dear friend. We wanted to be in a mentally stimulating space while we discussed recent ideas we both were mulling over. It was the perfect venue and our conversation has stuck with me since, like a scratching in the back of my head.

A long time ago,
in a small and nondescript
room, I cried to play,

and from outside the
window, the flowers and trees
asked, *Are you okay?*

Flipped and tricked
lickety-split
bicycles riding the clouds.

Round and round
up and down
handlebars leading the crowds.

Paths of grass
dogs and cats
seeds in fields to be plowed.

Sweeping brooms
empty rooms
silently screaming aloud.

Acts of creation
change who we are at our core,
so let go and build.

If you've ever been to a museum, looked at a piece of art, and thought to yourself, *this is stupid. I could create this*, you're not alone.

How you interpret art is subjective. It's subjective because you incorporate your experience, your beliefs, your ideology, and then project it onto the art. It's not bad to recognize and accept. After all, **this is how you engage with much of the world:** ***through your personal lens***.

When you see a work of art, and it resonates with you, what do you begin to consider? What do you think about the life of the artist? Do you think about what the artist felt during their art creation?

There is no right or wrong way to look at art. There is no right or wrong art. Art simply is, and you take it as you take many things around you.

Art is the mirror
through which we see reflections
beyond space and time.

The Logos calls us
from beyond the endless void
to act, create, live.

The Greeks believed in something called Logos. The Logos was an all-pervading force that controlled and directed both individuals and the universe as a whole. It was this ethereal power and an actual substance called pneuma (noo-ma) which some believed to be fire, and other Stoics believed to be a mix of fire and air, like a vital breath animating all living creatures.

It was the word, the reason, the plan that ordered the cosmos and gave form and meaning.

This concept is found in Persian and Indian theology and early Christianity: the logos was the foundation for God and for Jesus Christ.

Think to the first chapter in the book of Genesis, where the *word* of God, the *logos* of God, created heaven and earth.

And in Judaism, some scholars say the pronunciation of God is an audible out-breath.

I was raised in a culture where winning is everything. Or at least, that is what a child learns when they see the joy of a winner televised and broadcast everywhere. And what about the fury of the loser (who is going to come back!) you ask? Well, what do you think about when you hear the word loser? It's something no one *wants* to be.

So, you're either the thing that everyone loves (and envies?), or the thing no one wants to be.

Where is the room for those who want to learn?

Do not play to win,
play because it's good to play
for playing is fun.
And ultimately, you will
reduce your perfectionism.

Perfectionism is
the killer of hopeful dreams.
Don't believe me? Well,
try to be perfect and see
where you stand when the dust clears.

If only it were so simple…

To be a whale
whooshing through 3D space
pointed up and out
blasting into a new domain—
a Breach of conscious reality.

What a way to change perspectives.

How incredible it is
to know there is a world
on the other side
of space you can only visit.

And to think
all manner of men and women
have grown out of the mind
to breach a reality
we like to call home.

The complexity of it is astounding.
For who but children can leave this world
on a whim to chase dragons
or gnomes, or fairies, or talking rabbits.

We are troubled for losing sight
of how simple it once was
and how simple it still is.

Follow the calling,
that contagious excitement–
it's your energy.

There are some artists who think that they do not create
art themselves, that the art speaks through them.

Steven Pressfield, a writer who I look up to, says that he
speaks for the Muses, a group of women from ancient
Greek mythology who inspire literature, science, and art.

To Pressfield, the Muses are real,
because he believes they are real.

Whomever or whatever you think is helping you create
your art and helping you play, the source of your
creativity,
protect it.

The ultimate form
of the Source is how you work
your art, from pure play.

The dance builds up a wave crashing thirst
the water volts your body with an energy burst
bolting into the ocean becoming one with the earth
splashing ripples bow out with some friends immersed–
in the good times that you have together
birds of a feather
the weather above our heads has never been better
lunacy brings about utopian pleasure
as we travel and conquer this spinning spaceship
unfettered.

Silly humor, joy,
passion, courage, ferocious
curiosity—

with traits so great, no
surprise growing up is tough.
Blast maturity!

I'll speak for a large portion of people when I say:

don't give your kid a trophy for losing
(*encourage their efforts and support their continued work*)

don't force your kid to play in a specific way
(*let your kid lead playtime and adventures*)

don't always solve your kid's problems
(*guide them with questions and prompts to solve shit themselves*)

don't refrain from sharing stories about your life with
your kid for fear that it will teach them a bad lesson
(*articulate the stories of your life so your kid can learn through you*).

The surprise as a
kid, to learn skills, hear stories–
blissful paradigm.

SECTION 2:
PAIN AND LOSS

In the same way that you know it is night by contrast to the day, you know joy and success by means of understanding pain and loss.

Much of life is painful. Much of life is filled with loss. We all experience the same pain and loss in shades. And it's wonderful to see more popular voices speaking up about their pain and loss. I hope this trend continues.

You cannot tell them
the taste of it when they never
practiced artistry.
version 1

version 2
You cannot tell them
the taste of it when they never
practiced artistry.
Spells cast like springtime sunshine
when minds forget words exist.

I wrote this next poem when I was really depressed. It's a spoken poem.

I'm going to keep smiling...
Because most of our lives will be riddled with pain. Hearing that we're not good enough has almost been engraved in our brains, and although that always breaks our heart to hear, the amount of times it's been true are never clear.

Because most of the time we create that very illusion, not knowing enough to fight off the intrusion, that the only person who actually brings us down is ourselves, echoing the words of others against the cages walls, now becoming so enthralled and feeling like we'll fall, we're jumping around like a bouncing ball.

We become so detached from real life, plunging down cinematic emotional water slides where we feel like we can confide, because it's more clear with that box in Blu-ray and HD than out here with blue jays in 3D, not really using our eyes to actually see the compassion we receive.

We want to be fed information from streams, refusing to wake ourselves and attempt to live out our dreams, stuck in that trance of an artificial coma, being now a grownup without actually having grown up, think you made me throw up...

But I'm going to keep smiling...
Because of that feeling you get when you walk into a room, all eyes on you in center view, worrying if they're staring and laughing with your enemies and clapping at your expense. Feeling the need for a defense so you can lash out, with liquid courage you're brash now, but you're mumbles and mutters are trash now, incoherently flashing out—you're blacking out, waking in your room wondering why you feel so crappy now...

19

I no longer accept when people throw me in turmoil. I have watched the truth uncoil after they treated me like a royal, being defeated and stuffed up like a fat toad, their attitude so cold, sitting in cool water being brought to a slow boil, and I fought to not soil my limbs, not playing games on their whims, with lame blames they make me cringe. I'm no longer on the fringe of their cries, I've binged out their petty lies...

And I'm going to keep smiling...

Because we can prioritize where the first thing that comes out on the news is the truth, and reorganize our educational system to help develop the youth. Setting examples of mindfulness and restraint against the deceptions inducing pain. We were not put here with all of our differences to conform to a uniform state of mind, stop the blind leading the blind.

We must refrain from a self-loathing society, call it a bullshit sobriety, with no labels to trample and trip over, fiending for the fable we sampled with our wit molder—feeling bolder and bolder we can now smolder the opposition, trust me and take me up on my proposition.

Because we can keep smiling...

A shared word:
Indignation.
I ask why:
Agitation.
Ego so large
and wall so high,
recognition
gasps for air
and dies.

Receive words:
Trepidation.
You ask why:
Hesitation.
Fearing pain
with arms
open.

Heart spoken.

Pressure
rising pulse.
A thought
thought too close.
Offense
knowingly made.
A thought
feeling of blame.
Empathy
desire relief.
A thought
heartbeat increase.
Gift
deed accepted.
A thought
a thought corrected.

Listen and receive
soulful thoughts
expression unlaced
from intricate knots.

Rephrase not repeat
to understand
from where this
fiery spirit began.

Simple in needs
to each propose
best not to knock
down the domino.

Faced with the same
from first exploded
new knowledge tells
how best avoided.

Of joy,
of pain,
it's only humane–
eyes misbehave
tears do invade.

A feeling expressed
with thoughts undressed,
why keep writing if
doubt crawls around my neck?

Am I able to accomplish what
feels like an impossible mission?
When hiding from reality
becomes the accepted religion?

Is a fear of failure a common
thought among the peers?
Have I isolated and imagined
doubt for soundless cheer?

Who is it that I'm writing for?
Who is it I aim to support?
How do I know if my aid
has helped others transform?

Dedicated souls
embrace warm loving arms, now
left open to pain.

I fit in, I get lost.
I open up, I feel soft.

What need to be firm?
What need to be hard?
What need to be a man,
with emotions on guard?

I enjoy solitude
and sharing a story.
I enjoy when the hero
has vulnerable glory.

I will not conform
I demand to explore,
pursuing exchange of value
on a candid platform.

I'm powerful and emotional
a sensitive and gentle man.
I'm authentic in action
to myself truly genuine.

Mirror, mirror, parallel life —
have reflections passed us by?

Who can say what is here is not more beautiful
than the other side?

The birds arise with
the steam of morning dew.
The fawn and mother

Scavenge, as starlight
pierces leaves and branches. The wind
carries scent and sound.

With little pause,
embracing with each pass.

The living and non-living, not all concepts
exist through action shaping purpose.

Dreams realized from plans,
plans achieved with goals,
goals moved accomplished with steps,
steps executed with acts,
acts with movement attain life.

In our changing world,
no two wind gusts are the same–
some shout, some whisper.

Learning to walk
we stumble and fall,
lifting ourselves back up
and attempting another step.
And we fall—
and again, and again we fall,
until one day,
we can hold ourselves on one leg.
Yet we do not stand still,
we step with the momentum.
The balancing act
is not to balance in stillness,
it is to balance in movement.
It is the trick we forget,
that to learn to walk
we continue to fall forward,
catching ourselves with every step.
Surely we fall again,
and again, and again we fall.
Yet we continue to stand,
to try once more,
for we are not meant to stop,
we are meant to push forward,
to push onward.
We will use our momentum,
and continue to fall.

We are moving forward,
we are falling forward,
with each step.

Flowing rocks, rigid
water — trees lining up for
the morning slaughter.

Murders of sheep and
herds of crows — teeth fall out like
dental dominos.

Chaotic peace, and
simplistic wars — hands swapped for
claws can't open doors.

Reflection people
mirror culture, as art helps
raise fruitful sculptors.

Circut waves leading
tidal boards, mysterious
life seems quite ignored.

Some time in 2018, I started having some pain in my hip. Having previously worked in the fitness industry, I was surrounded by very knowledgeable people, so with their help, I figured out a way to feel better. Then the pain came back. So I went to specialists, then doctors, then surgeons.

In the end, I discovered my back was broken. A vertebrae shattered, and the spinal disk beneath this shattered bone also ruptured. So, with free-floating broken bones and a degenerative disk, I live on.

I stretch a lot. I'm careful with my workouts. I don't lift heavy, anymore. I even identified a few things that agitate the pain, and I avoid those things.

And still, sometimes, I experience nerve pain so powerful, that on a scale of

❖ 1-10, where 10 is I cannot walk, it's an easy 10
❖ 1-10, where 10 is I want to kill myself, it's a 7 or 8 (the instances when this happens have decreased because of the work I put into keeping limber)

I haven't received the *corrective* surgery yet. There are many reasons why, and there are many reasons why one day I will get the surgery.

The pain slows me down physically and mentally. The pain gives me space to reassess my life and activities.

And this pain, it's unique. There is nothing else in my life where, semi-regularly, I have the opportunity to really stop and consider what pain means or what it does to the mind and body. In many ways, and in growing ways by the year, I am acquainted with pain again and again.

I don't fear pain, even if it still sucks, every time.

Once strong
feeling weak,
stinging pain
twisted physique,
walking hurts
mindset defeat,
research commences
reason mystique.

Willful mind
body swollen,
innards twinge
track chosen,
coming growth
heart unbroken,
painful steps
passing moments.

SECTION 3:
LOVE AND ROMANCE

Reflecting back, it was my need to feel loved that drove me to do and learn so many things. Funny enough, these things usually resulted in me falling in love with the unexpected. For example:

❖ I picked French over Spanish as the language to study in middle school because I heard a rumor the girl I crushed on was going to study French. The rumor was false, and I had an opportunity to fall in love with the language.

❖ I wanted to play with my brother when he had friends over. They were older and stronger, so when play was rough, I would get hurt and cry. My mom would comfort me, my brother apologetic (sometimes), and both she and he would say, "he just needs a thicker skin, he's sensitive." So, I started to repress my feelings to be *tough*. This choice I made to be tough put me on the sidelines a lot when it came to friendships, best to remove myself and emotions so they're not a burden to others, and at the same time, I was given the opportunity to fall in love with people watching.

❖ I sought a deeper connection with one ex-girlfriend who told me she wanted to study psychology in college, so I purchased a psychology textbook and read it. The plan was to talk about psychology with her. In my studies, I had the opportunity to fall in love with the human mind.

We often choose to do things based on what's going on around us. It's only natural.

Within this section is a series of poems using very similar metaphors and imagery. Sometimes, artists will work through a series in an attempt to find the perfect form, knowing they will always fall short of perfect, and still striving to find it nonetheless. This series is dedicated to that pursuit, the love we discover along the way, and

a mermaid.

Earth to moon to sun,
you'll find the timeless flowers
blooming between lips.

Upon my boat I've sailed the seas,
the seven oceans I've felt their breeze.

But once I laid my eyes on you,
I fell in love that much is true.

The moonlit sky upon your face,
the mermaid tail you wave with grace.

I wave hi back and a smile appears,
on my lips from ear to ear.

A creature with beauty just like yours,
drives pirates to plunder in treasure troves.

And gifts the sun a set at night,
so stars may shine with their own light.

You're on my mind all night and day,
upon my chest I wish you lay.

And soon we will embrace again,
for you are my dearest and closest friend.

Cultivate love's soil:
watering seeds and plucking
weeds—discussing needs.

I bite my cheek because of nerves.
My chest beats hard against your curves.
You cry to me you dislike to surface.
Wading in water lungs full of purpose.

In your domain, release the ecstasy.
Staring in your eyes, a dark recipe.
Losing mind, catching breath we see,
underwater with you is the death of me.

Exploring the black, sights adjust to mind.
Love pressure wraps around us in kind.
Gills and fins grow, our lives entwine.

Down here with you, I breathe and am no longer blind.

Words from love are the
universal way to send
messages through time.

Resting on the sand
toes curling tiny grains,
memory of your lips
kissing edges of my brain.

Eyes orbit 'round the ocean
dreaming of your next surface,
time between our meetings
weighs heavy like a tortoise.

Circled by laughing people
engaged in sunny action,
I'm fixed upon the water
longing for your silky passion.

Last embrace we held had
attuned my mind with yours,
sowing luscious inclinations
and a craving in my core.

To love and to be loved,
you can never give up.

Frustration brews with family —
how many times have I asked you this?
How many times do I need to say?
Why do we always revisit this cliche?

Yet it is with family, however you define that—
where I feel the safest,
where I feel the most heard,
where feelings of support are assured.

Too many relationships gone sour —
power slipping from my hand,
records show it doesn't last,
my mind dumped is a wasteland.

Yet exposure to pain is an antenna for love —
the value of mountains tops is the knowledge of ditches,
wounds stitched I continue to fight,
knowing the end is filled with delight.

Friends, family, or something more —
to pursue passion we take risks,
to conquer suffering we unveil emotions,
we will love again and are not broken.

To love and to be loved,
you can never give up.

Scooped up by winds too
turbulent, Cupid's wings beat
harder than permanence.

You sent a message to me this morning
the rising tides convey your story,
jealousy seething of my time on land
how dare I be what I am, a man.

Your wish for me to live with you
within the water with gratitude
has been received and dare I say
the gills still need a little airway.

I long to swim the ocean current
a leatherneck turned marine merchant,
but with legs, I also long to walk the sand
why for that must I be damned?

I'm never so far away from the ocean.
I'll come back soon to convey my devotion.
You are my stars, you are my sun,
my mind and heart for you are one.

Sadness for the king
abandoned by the queen
all
imagined in a dream.

Confused but transported
forgetting catastrophic distortion
to
a waking world euphoric.

Memories bubble
she and I are a couple
and
this nightmare is no trouble.

The truth pulled through
reality construes

P.S.
I love you.

Adorable mix
quickly scooped up, stranger's pup,
unlimited licks,
unconditional love–then
returned back in kind. Full stop.

A trip planned with you,
beach meetings after adieu,
carried softly by sunbeams,
darkness runs from our dreams,
excitement washing over my hands,
feet covered from deep digs in sand,
graciously you wade in deep water,
hoping I come out much farther,
invited by your bubbling eyes,
jumping in water revived,
kisses no longer wait,
Oh loving mermaid.

Love is something you are given and give.

Love is not something to take.

Forget this
and lose

your

way.

Difficulties alive–
in your eyes I see frustration.
Mistakes made and
attempts to rectify pervade,
happiness for first tiffs find
cracking smiles hide,
acknowledge I
apologize.

Can I wade in waters you reside?
Am I allowed to feel absolved if I
have tried to make all parties rise
in the face of darkness?

One stream becomes overflowing rapids.
I've landed in deeper waters
then I can handle.
Longing to lean
on you for
assistance
your anger
creates
resistance.

I tire of treading,
I need you
again,
please
pardon my
miscommunication.

Modern-day telepathy
by way of circuits and chips
shooting invisible waves,
how has fortune not favored
those living today?

Burdened with zeal
I find myself looking in your direction
wonderfully curious,
do you know my heart lives
for the waves?

Seasonal change has
provoked the currents
to provide for you a gift,
one of intangible
metrics.

My spirit and strength
encouraging enthusiasm
matching your vivacity,
our bond has been
serendipitous.

How far we've come
in such a short time
as I stand on the bank
of the Ocean's tide.

The rocks are lapped
and crushed by waves—as
your words ensnare,
your kiss enslaves.

There's Chaos in our minds,
to believe two beings
so alike
could ever come from different sides.

And yet we stand as evidence
the elegance of love's recklessness
has been quite generous
to our genesis.

A lovely benefit
we dared to be degenerate.

These have been difficult times,
laden with heavy thoughts,
away from water, from sand,
from a space you love.

Let me be your solace,
a place where your mind
may swim freely.

Free, within the vastness
of our relationship.

We are an ocean
through our acceptance.

We are a hurricane
through our emotions.

We are a tidal wave
through our actions–
Together.

We are not to be trifled with,
for we are more with each other
than we have ever been
without.

Our warmth was built through the cracks of the ocean floor
in complete darkness, cold, pressured despair,
when we explored the other's life
and history.

Our hurricane gathered force
when we shared openly
what we needed,
what we wanted,
and how the
other may
help.

Our tidal wave formed
when the decision was made
to be together through any storm.

May we always build this earthly force
that feels so natural so long as we promise to be

Unapologetically,
Empathetically,
Acceptingly,
Loving.

Beneath the waves, a mermaid awaits,
her beauty capturing all who gaze,
the spark of love I dare not deny,
my heart it soared, I made up my mind.

No matter the consequence,
I'd give up my common sense,
for such joy is paired with salty-eyed strife,
as dreams of us together flicker in the night.

No land would she have, no castle near,
she chose a life instead so deep and clear,
our journey to find space we both could stay,
within time we saw our love found its way.

Upon the shore each night and then,
a siren's song she sang again,
and longing grew with passing day,
our forbidden love like the sun's bright ray.

Get lost, they yelled to
the boy's back, for they didn't know
that his companion,
that his love, already left.
He was as lost as they come.

Clouds brewing above our heads
where no one thought to glance,
our focus was on the other
in the fields on which we danced.
Recall the first date as a cloudy joy
like an eloquence storm
"The world is a cold place," I replied,
good company will keep us warm.
The clouds were wisps at first
hard to see even if you looked,
as time together evaporated
we missed that we were hooked.
Puffs of cloud clumped together
slowly building mass,
your animation entertains
when you compliment my ass.
Clumpy clouds became dark and heavy
as the drizzle came dripping down,
I drew you in under umbrellas
where our bond was safe and sound.
The clouds grew large and dangerous
with lightning strikes and thunder,
our relationship was on the edge
our words had developed a hunger.
So clouds released their burdened weight
and overwhelmed our cover below,
soaked hand-in-hand *I Love You*
cleared the sky for a wondrous rainbow.

SECTION 4:
ACTS AND PERFORMANCE

I took acting classes for about a year at Susan Batson Studios. I'm unsure how I initially heard about it or what prompted me to attend my first class, though I always had a good time. Many classes started with everyone in a circle, with one person entering the circle at a time. This person in the middle would then make noise, say something, move their body, or combine any of these things. Then, everyone around the circle would need to copy them.

It gave people an opportunity to let loose at the beginning of class. It gifted people a space, void of judgment, to act out any frustrations they might have been holding. And, it also answered the question: *what exactly does this person in the middle of the circle want to express?*

At times, the person's verbal or behavioral expression felt primal. Other times the expression was suppressed, as if they couldn't get past themselves, as if they were a puppet to their darkness, dancing on the strings of their

61

fears.

Ms. Batson wrote *Truth: Personas, Needs, and Flaws in the Art of Building Actors and Creating Characters*. With an introduction by Nicole Kidman, a student of Ms. Batson's particular style of method acting, this book serves as a unique look into what it takes to act, to become a character.

We all play a character in the story of life. You play a character with your friends, with your family, with your coworkers. Sometimes, the characters you play are similar. Sometimes they are different.

Do you know who your character is? What are their motivations? What do they desire in your story?

If you don't know, ask the character what their story is, and what drives them to act. Not act as in pretend. Act as in move. Act as in action.

Rocket fuel with precision
is the most effective decision.
Light some fuel in a bucket
watch intense explosives trumpet.

Light the same fed to fight gravity
propulsion systems conquer casually.
Identify fuel and focus energies
watch yourself flourish ever so steadily.

Bearing the weight of existence,
demand your ambition
to face and conquer resistance.

Funding assets
real estate
influence games
and masquerades.

To muse
on cause
price rise
scream applause.

Falling down
action rueful
chief moral
capital Brutal.

Evolution's pace
speeding f o r w a r d, liable

to flip any moment.

Change is a constant
making life feel like a monster,
if you're unwilling to accept
adapting is required to prosper.
Ideas are not part of our personality,
they are concepts to evolve,
if one idea isn't working
there will be another idea of resolve.
Those choosing to improve are
perceived as dismissing the old,
but as times change, different
problems demand a different mold.
Changing rules, changing games,
moving shots with moving aim,
abandoning guilt, dissolving shame,
not a tight box, but a light frame.

Crisp and clear, flying
through the atmosphere, leaving
behind doubt and drear.

There is a long road ahead,
feelings of fear and dread
whirling dizzy in my head.

I'm not actually drowning.
I can climb this mountain,
for this anxiety is grounding.

Preparation diligent,
synchronizing vigilance —
systemization significance.

Stepping upon the first stair
imaginary voices aim to scare
declaring reality a nightmare.

Yet light beams on horizons,
dissolving gloom into silence.
This is the resolve uprising.

Tasks complete — rejoice!
Success finds voice
ascending the noise.

Broken, shattered, beaten, defeated,
rebuilt stronger, beautiful, achieving freedom.

Rise before the sun, with the moon still up high,
a lunar sunrise in disguise—so beautiful to my eyes,
when the cosmic entity of light brightens the sky,
is when all life wills to arise.

And the plants they do confide
they wish to grow and expand,
unaware of the concerns of man
no surprise they don't understand,
holding power and delicacy,
like a glass cannon.

One foot down,
one foot up,
falling forward keeps us from hitting

the ground.

Choose warmth–for a smile
builds heat, like kindling for a
kind community.

Choose growth–for lessons
learned today skip past troubles
we meet tomorrow.

Choose tomorrow–for
today's foundation was built
by you, yesterday.

Spoken silently with a body of love
'I'm here for you should you need, my friend.'

The challenges
of addiction,
beaten back with company
warm
and eager to fight.

Cheek kisses and hugs, pats on back, proud joyful eyes,
'you're on the right path.'

Immobilized by fear, by weight so hefty and
invisible,
no one believed it was there.

But no one asked for belief,
The request was for support.

'I'm here for you when you need, my friend,'
is enough.

Distractions and noise,
babble of everyday life,
memories echo.

Overwhelmed by thoughts,
is a bridge safe when built void
of all mindfulness?

'Muddy water is
best cleared by leaving it be,'
thank you Alan Watts.

The bed beckons
our clothes hug,
the loser's lesson lost
to grinning mugs.

Lectures fall neutral
for all to relish,
gobbled as brutal
embellished angelics.

Beseeching dirty hands
paused minds, distilled thoughts,
friends of action weaving words,
connecting dots.

Comfort dazes
enervating spry masses,
rendering projects
hesitant and impassive.

So where do sloths look
when even comfort becomes too little,
when all the world was there for them
but now their crystal castles fizzle.

To further comfort!
for times are trying and oppress,
they say, the world's against me
and I can make no more progress!

To scriptures I look
for fate is in the hands of another,
for all of life I can't control
as Zeus commands the sound of thunder.

And so this sloth who threw
their hands up in tholing gloom
sits beneath the sound of rain
accepting the thunder as their doom.

Which direction
can be seen as the better
when roads end
beyond sight and
comprehension?

Which voice
can be seen as the greater
when volumes differ,
and perspectives range
broadly?

Which future
can be seen as the grander
when the hereafter
isn't lived, it's
envisioned?

Which choice
can be seen as *the* choice?
Who can say?
Only you can
decide.

Embracing heat as
leaves change, a fire ignites to
burn like velvet silk.

To play, fail, learn, grow
action across forever,
lost to inert souls.

Yet to pause, stillness,
expands certain pleasure found
with refined balance.

So walk, trip, enjoy
the climb, for each peak has views
verve souls can savor.

The path was long, difficult,
laden with obstacles, twists, and turns.

Following your light,
you may begin to feel like your shadow,
for the path is only visible to you with light or without,
and only you know where it leads.

"Where can I go?"
comes your question.
Where do you want to go?
comes the reply.

Upon finding the answer,
you begin to follow your spirit,
clearing new paths,
crossing clearings without trails.

And every crossroads you find,
every trailhead you mark,
and every choice you make,
will take you in new directions.

It is not death we fear,
it is the unknown.

Be strong,
be brave,
believe in your choices.
believe in your spirit to guide your life.

Ears ringing,
phantom vibrations,
the noise fills your mind.
Pulled left and right,
away, and yet toward
a love of unknowns.
Pings and pause,
hearts flutter from
worry and excitement,
who dares to risk it all?
Ears twitch,
tactile sensations,
quivering thoughts
beg for mercy.
Does the Siren
win the day?
Is the luscious sound
sincerely so strong?
Who dares to call
From the other side,
where dreams never breathe
and nightmares sleep,
dreaming of different lands?
To call back,
a warrior's cry,
daring the void
to enter your mind.

Fear.
Reverence.
Qualms.
Confidence.

Heroes rises against inner gravity
to resolve external calamity.

Movement of free rain,
drops of new life gently wash
exposed earth, to mud.

Then rain becomes a
river, raging through landscapes
amidst pleasant groves.

Fear is a morphing concept,
a concept that seeks to limit
your actions and ambitions.
Fear is the voice inside your head saying
you will not succeed,
you cannot overcome,
you are not worthy,
you lack intelligence,
you're not meant to be here.
Fear is the rationalization of
the outcome was out of my control,
it was not my fault,
it was their fault we failed,
if only they listened to me,
no one could complete this feat.
Fear is the gravity pulling you down and back when
you seek redemption,
you search for answers and solutions,
you hunt for knowledge,
you labor toward growth.
Fear is walking on a beach
with sand clutched in your hand
complaining you have to hold it.
Fear is turning on the television
with a blindfold over your eyes
complaining you cannot see.
Fear is the debilitating idea
you choose to feed
because you believe it protects you,
from a potential you.

Have you ever thought the
thought, *could this be all there is?*
If not, I envy you.
If yes, fret less, for you're not
alone,

not *absolutely*.

Striving towards perfection was the idea
passed down from generation to generation,
and the truth remained hidden.

The straightest lines in the universe,
parallel to one another,
will curve a little as they near the weight of a star.

Perfection was not meant to be reached,
we hold our wits about us as we walk next to perfection,
not toward it.
To acknowledge perfection as a concept
never meant to become reality,
is to see the invisible wall between you and imagination.

How much of our imagination bleed through the cracks?
Who can say or know
besides the one who imagines?

You were born when you did not ask to be.
You were brought into this world
based on someone else's choice.

And now,
you are here.

Your family, your friends, the people who
support you in your endeavors
seek to help, to assist
somehow.

How much help can they provide
if *you* have not decided to help *yourself?*

The world is not here to make your life easy
it is not here to clear you a path
it is not here for
you.

Here, you are among many.
Here, you are in many ways
alone.

Who lives within your reality?
Who has been with you all your life?
Who knows all there is to know about *you?*
When will you decide you will help *yourself?*

You will always be your first hero.
You will always be the first to say
help me.
Here is my hand,
can someone help?

This is *you*, supporting *you*,
seeking support from others.

You make the decisions for your life.
You take action on your own accord.
You create your reality.

And everything you've ever wanted for yourself
is up to *you*
to find
to obtain
to achieve
to be.

You will struggle,
you will fail,
and *you* will find a way
to get back up.

Your possibilities are based on *your* actions.
Your actions are based on *your* thoughts.
Your thoughts are based on *your* resolve.

Head high
project ready,
verbal hurdles
palms sweaty,
skills set
purpose hefty,
present well
praise merrily.

Time passes
pilot prepared,
world changes
plan impaired,
freeze momentum
discourage flares,
top-down
stop declared.

Awaiting arrival
for you, as the morning dew
rests upon the grass,

anticipating
the heat of the sun, to rise
once more into air.

Sensing elation!
To be free from the tethers
of our gravity.

It begins with a seed,
hard and small.
Covered in dirt and debris,
it appears stuck.
Does it accept this fate?
Does it give up?
No.

Seeking out nutrients
from the surrounding area,
the seed wants to grow.

We do not know
what flower the seed
will become.
Will it be a rose?
Will it become a poppy?
The mystery remains
unsolved, so long as the
flower is not nurtured.

The seed will remain
hard, small, and seemingly stuck
should *no one* come
and aid its growth.

A storm may come,
battering rain and
clashing lightning.

We imagine the seed is helpless,
and yet, it seeks out nourishment,
growing from the storm
in impossible odds.

The storm has passed,
the flower has sprouted,
and here comes the sun.
A bright and vibrant life
warmed by light.

The seed held strong,
still, but strong, against
the storm, against the
odds, against what seemed to be
the world pouring down.

How are we the seed?
How are we to be nourished?
What can we do against impossible
odds, when it seems like the world
is against us?

We hold still.
We seek nourishment,
and sun, and water.

For we must water the seed
to see the flower.

One face is for the public,
to show to others
to be perceived
to live life covered
and well received.

One face is for loved ones,
to share ourselves
to feel connection
to gift our mind
from introspection

One face is for ourselves,
to safe keep secrets
to hide some flaw
to shelter an ego
from reality's jaw.

We all wear a face,
and the more connected
each face is to the other
the more united we feel
the less we are to suffer.

SECTION 5:
EVERYDAY OBSERVATIONS

The world is a beautiful place. It's hard to recognize this when in pain, when dealing with loss, or honestly, just in general.

Sometimes all we need to do to remember this, that the world is a beautiful place, is for someone to point out a simple thing that catches our eye.

You can also train yourself to notice these things and be the person who *points out*.

That can be you.

Inside or without
each moment, as beautiful
as the last one felt.

Vessel built
singular purpose
retaining heat
delicious worship.

Inside cardboard
cheesy bread
saucy endorphins
tomato spread.

Carried far
destination known
ring doorbell
sometimes phone.

Box opened
content produced
tossed away
station absolute.

Be open to the
lightning strikes
and the mundane,
because you can have an
extraordinary life
from ordinary moments.

Long walks, small talk.
Hi, hello, how are you?
Carry the weight by day.
Questions come late at night.

Feet move, sound grooves.
Good, thanks, see you later.
Rise each day to be stronger.
Who's dream is this racing onward?

New song, sing along.
Wow, sweet, you're an artist.
Seek a challenge and then conquer.
Strive to live life with courage and honor.

Waves crash
seagulls squawk
gritty sand
crunching walk
loving voices
memory swells
when listening
to the shell.

Even a broken
shell whispers the secrets of
life, if you listen.

Moldy flower.
dirty dishes.
mornings without kisses.
Cleaning now.
request plans.
lovers holding hands.
Lies told.
not forgotten.
relations gone rotten.
Lonely now.
despise weeping.
begin friendship seeking.
Knowing self.
hobbies align.
communication is divine.
Feeling good.
mindset matches.
fishing lure catches.
First meet.
slightly shy.
with compassionate eyes.
Get along.
meet mates.
love language translates.
Take risk.
express affection.
she reciprocates connection.

Resting eyes where dreams take flight, thoughts crystallize
within twilight, all to satisfy sleep's appetite.

A chase
running in place
chest pounding
yes
death awaits.

Zombies
monsters
goons and ghouls
physics holds
no rules.

Stabbed and scratched
silent screaming
a shooting pain
I must

be dreaming.

Thirst to stir
brought to mind
a strong stench
with the orderly grind.

The faucet runs
clear and neat
as I prepare
the dawning treat.

The glass sits empty
awaiting the period
when liquid returns
dark and mysterious.

Excitement brewed
behind eyes still glossy
with a sip of the hot
black morning coffee.

Breathing in nighttime heat
scanning stars already passed
lover's hands long for each other
summer comes and goes so   fast.

Feel how your ideas
can flow through you, running like
eternal rivers.

Puffs of heavy air
Distort sight, operation
Serendipitous.

Sometimes flavor
often heat
despising you
saucy treat.

Pizza additive
spaghetti paste
fair cuisine
an acquired taste.

Indian staple
Italian element
lovely band
but sweaty requisite.

"Hot in —
hot out,"
mothers words
ring doubt.

Initiate bonding!
Raising libido?
One day
little peperoncino.

Weathered and
worn, a world with
endless movement grows
resilient and stronger
with each crack.

When solitude becomes the norm
questions we thought were never born
clearly bear no fruitful tour
to imagine a time without distracting swarms.

A spot for quiet and simple space
in retirement we all do chase
for tides of fate rock our base
and perturbation remains our state.

The words of prophets old and new
recurring themes are gifts to you
delicious wines of royal blues
lessons gleaned with a thought corkscrew.

Now twist and turn to reside atop
these cloudy days which cease to stop
to cultivate a sunny thought
and water life like a bright raindrop.

Rough patches
tough matches.

Pronounced frilled
breezey chill.

Delicate brush
skin flush.

Warm smother
altered color.

Moisture union
contact illusion.

Blazing surge
animation purge.

Spooning pressure
feeling better.

Welcomed gesture
human texture.

Cue hullabaloo—
blooming dino fields gyp lore
gambolling about,

tele creation
to organize waffling hats
and laden ladders.

What will you do when you realize the lie? The lie we
have all been told, over and over,
and over once more.

Will you be able to accept it?
Will you confront yourself and know it to be true?
Will it matter most to you?
Will things change when the trust bares its plain face?

Indeed, for the truth is plain and we imagine it ugly or
beautiful. We turn nothing into things and
things into nothing.

Can you feel the tension inside rising?
It is a visceral feeling–
disgust for ideology held,
frustration for having been tricked,
sadness for those who suffered,
resentment towards those who knew,
happiness for now knowing.

But what next? What can be done? Abandon ship?
Renovate? Redesign? Overthrow? Depart the party?

Opinions on which move is better swarm our extelligence
like locusts on the horn of Africa.

The season of change is upon us, or rather,
it never left.

Flames flicker,
numbering many
movements separate
directions plenty.

Knee down
flame fades
smoke rising
flickers enraged.

Stand together
flickers soar
united heat
blazing roar.

Together again
single direction
focused aim
laser progression.

Stomach full craving sweets,
caffeine too, delectable
treat—consumed quickly.

Linear waves and cyclical events,
there's a capital growing on the present's instants.

Experiential dollops through backward perception,
Reversing forward was the immaculate conception.

From pygmy lightning strikes and
twisting pikes with growing and shrinking distance,
evolutions from great-grandchildren of mountains mixed
with manmade molten infants.

What turns the mind from one conception to another,
if not for the clicks and hums of the nutrient crusher?

Priming and prompting, there's no human immune
to the presence of a detachment-mirage thought attitude.

If change occurs indefinitely,
does anything change
from the changing state?
Perpetually crashing
into a stale freedom.

Slowing building
a tension tsunami
a mind's battle
for control of a body.

Fingers shaking
and arms twitch
a body's cue
for a mind bewitched.

Was it coffee this morning
or a meeting upcoming?
The heart is pounding
the foot tap drumming.

Electric signals
revive inert metal plates
and pulse on the atoms
of evolved primates.

Stand up.
Breath deeply.
Cliche? Sure,
but it works completely.

Indications, signs,
prompts, and signals—
high systems spinning
so we may juggle the riddles.

The idea of splicing, whether with RNA or rope, is to join two pieces together that were not connected before. In the case of rope, the product of the splice is stronger than before.

Bring to mind the first part of splicing, which is to undo the items that will eventually create the lasting product.

Our culture, our world, is enduring the *undoing* phase of splicing. I believe we will join together in the end (call it optimism) to become better, together.

Strands disentangled, a mirage of disconnection–
then woven back, supporting more than before.

Push and pull, flower
petals falling like raindrops
on words cutting skin.

Who knew blades of grass
could embrace like silk bedsheets,
when entropy fell?

Emotions collapse,
a mind's erosion starting
fluid explosion.

A blooming culture
disillusioned enough–for
galvanized hatred

infects just kinship.
Lament, mourn, none of prudence
query rotten speech.

Tempting unsightly
visitors–Washington xanned
yesterday's zombies.

SECTION 6:
SPIRITUAL AND PHILOSOPHICAL

Humanity has a fascination with many things. Higher on the list than most is the spiritual and philosophical realm, with questions asked in years chief among the realm. Should one question not reach an answer, the next generation may ask the same question, or ask a new one; a variation.

The provoking thought about these questions is not whether we will ever find an answer, it is the curiosity of if the questions require an answer. And lest we forget the musing meditations, as if their beauty held anything less than the unanswerable questions.

Or something like that.

The reason we gaze
upon the ocean is to
see a true mirror
version 1

version 2
We gaze upon the
ocean to reflect our true
nature and being

Knowing one day you'll
pass through life's thin veil, to greet
an old friend named death
is all the force you should need
to focus on life today.

We are the river,
believing we lose a piece
of who we are
each time we adjust to
the environment around us.

Yet, this is not the case.

The river is a morphing, ambiguous shape.
The river is not the water lost to the land
with each adjustment.

Indeed, the river is the never-ceasing flow of water,
the totality of movement.

We do not lose ourselves as we grow, as we learn,
as we leave behind a piece of who we were.

We are the morphing, ambiguous shape we define
ourselves to be.

Dreams, waking moments,
both of them are just as real,
or unreal, in state.

We are like the prism—
neutral events enter in,
then fracture apart
to a spectrum of colors:
our thoughts, feelings, sensations.

Emotional maturity is recognizing and having the ability to stop reactions before they occur. *You do not have to react* to your environment, to the stimulus of your life and world.

Emotional wisdom is the ability to choose how you react to your environment, regardless of how much you like or dislike a thing. *You can choose what to think, what to say, what to do* in every moment.

When you know this to be true, you can choose.

Information surge
subliminal birth

cosmic pour
oron forge

twirling noggin
limbic caution

reverie knotted
rhythm hypnotic

insensible logic
living subconscious.

Release attachments
so that your life can arrive
in its truest form.

Measured for meaning we've become invested,
in building a life we value as impressive,
around an imaginary concept impossibly majestic.

The human tendency to seek meaning and purpose in life, while noble, has branched evolutions; some of which are beautiful, some of which are horrid. The emphasis on appearing impressive to others come from a dark place. It resolves around an imagined concept of what *should be*, that grand and unattainable, elusive *natural nature* defined by societal standards. And so, the struggle of life pulls between personal values and societal expectations.

A shell
hard
closed off, yet
resilient.
Patient
for opportunity's
moist kiss,
brilliance.
Cracked
budding
driven high, to
spotlight.
Pea green
struggling
to grow, with
delight.
Bloom unique
alone,
thought to be
damned.
Petals open
serene,
in a barren
wasteland.
Noise
not wind
in bound, a
bumblebee.
Elated
for potential
procured, with
company.

Light and darkness coexist
exuberant novas play a show
quantum ripples swiftly kiss
beyond event horizon's glow.

Looking up upon sterile luster
annihilation beckons forth
life may have roared a thunder
but death delights assured of birth.

Grim conclusions for
living creatures, the last stand
before the unknown.

Space and time
effortlessly expand
between breaths
on foreign land,

Frightful feelings
will dissipate
when opening
fears floodgate.

We paddle out to
greet the wave, discouraged the
surf forgot our tryst.

Now freely floating
on swells too small to carry
us—we paused in bliss.

Equanimity,
balanced on waves and stillness,
boundlessly patient.

The sea is full to the brim,
the sky rests lightly on her shoulders.

The mirror reflects the mind,
more perceiving than seeing minds.

Linen skin-wrapped day and night,
blades of grass cut rubber feet green.

Owls pluck mice under moonlight,
eagles catch fish under sun.

To rise and fall is one,
transitions played forward and backward.

To ask what in a world of who's
and to be turned away because the answer is —

Enough of a reason for action of being
for action of doing or seeing,

And if Failure is hated by —
why pretend nothing Fails at all?

What do you feel in a field of flowers
if when's and where's are all that matter?

A close-ended thinker sees little
difference in birds or airplanes.

An open-ended mind finds joy in a child's
ad infinitum why's.

Why raise limbs for fisticuffs
as if words don't communicate enough?

A spirit full of how's, what's, and why's
always seems to find bright skies,
beaming through eternal darkness.

Locked away,
yet I am free—
I am wherever
my mind takes me.

Electrically
alive, consciousness sprouts new
buds too curious

to be called finite–
but without purpose, reason,
time lost forever.

Where is your temple?
Where does it lay?
Where are the foundations
for the righteousness to pray?

Do they lay down the street?
A mile from home?
Must you be there in-person
for your heart to not roam?

As if it mattered
for all religions pass
but here we do not speak ill
of your beliefs or your brass.

What is the purpose?
What is the mission?
To be good and do good
or collide with heretics' vision?

Love thy neighbor,
Support the wretched,
do your morals and ethics
deem life to be precious?

More ways to fight
or reasons to be different
while pleas for help
drag on unlistened.

What religion,
of the new or the old?
Who says all allegories
believe they are gold?

Placeholders of space,

time, and community,
a thin veil that hides
life's non-exclusivity.

There is no difference
between you and your foe,
unless by miracle
the Gods make it so.

What religion?
To whom do you pray?
Does it matter if you
have not been good today?

I skim through the poems and articles written to realize
the same ideas continue to jump out again and again.

These are feelings and desires placed into words,
attempting to bewitch the reader,
modern-day telepathy,
from my mind to yours.

These ideas
of perspective,
of change and acceptance,
of failure and embrace,
of growth and adaptation,
of relationships and patience,
of deconstruction and love,
of life and space.

These ideas are adjusting.

These ideas are morphing
ambiguous shapes,
of contemplation and introspection,
held by our mind
for brief periods of time.

Until we decide to adjust again.

As a river adjusts its course,
changing
as the landscape changes.

EXPLORING FURTHER

Amazon: *Whispers In Time*

Post your feedback of this book on Amazon by leaving a comment/review. Your review means a great deal.

Word of Mouth: Tell your Friends

Share this book with friends or family members if you could collect some insight about yourself while reading my poems and stories.

Social: @kylenielson (IG) & @kylenielson_ (X)

Follow the story as it unfolds with the social media handles for Instagram and X (fna Twitter) above. You have an open invitation to send me direct messages or not, whatever you feel comfortable doing.

Book: *Sharing Treasure*
Read my first book, *Sharing Treasure*, to vicariously learn through lessons and reflects from the raw and unspoken parts of my life. Scan this QR code on the left to navigate to *Sharing Treasure*.

Podcast: *How You Level Up*
Listen to the podcast, *How You Level Up*, where I unpack timeless communication lessons to help you level up. The podcast is available on all podcasting platforms. Scan this QR code on the left navigate to the various podcast platforms.

Course: Free of Charge
Participate in my free courses on Udemy. Scan this QR code on the left to navigate to the current courses offered free of charge.

ABOUT THE AUTHOR

Kyle Nielson is a writer, a poet, an avid reader, a fitness enthusiast, and the host of *How You Level Up*. This podcast provides communication and soft skills education. He holds degrees in Communications (MA), Mass Communications, and Media (BA).

He served in the Marine Corps, has worked in relationship management for over 12 years, and negotiated millions of dollars in partnerships and sales. Kyle has cultivated a unique and strategic communication style with a breadth of knowledge from working in cybersecurity, real estate, ed-tech, healthcare, logistics, insurance, luxury services, and sports-tech.

In his free time, he researches topics such as ethics, linguistics, and ontology.

Leave a Review:
If you have enjoyed this book, please leave an honest review on Amazon. I greatly appreciate the review and so will other customers.

Made in the USA
Monee, IL
11 January 2024

50679071R00092